Keto Meal Prep Cookbook for Beginners

50+ Quick and Easy Recipes for Homemade Cooking

Isabelle Young

Disclaimer

The information contained i is meant to serve as a comprehensive collection of strategies that the author of this eBook has done research about. Summaries, strategies, tips and tricks are only recommendation by the author, and reading this eBook will not guarantee that one's results will exactly mirror the author's results. The author of the eBook has made all reasonable effort to provide current and accurate information for the readers of the eBook. The author and it's associates will not be held liable for any unintentional error or omissions that may be found. The material in the eBook may include information by third parties. Third party materials comprise of opinions expressed by their owners. As such, the author of the eBook does not assume responsibility or liability for any third party material or opinions. Whether because of the progression of the internet, or the unforeseen changes in company policy and editorial submission guidelines, what is stated as fact at the time of this writing may become outdated or inapplicable later.

TABLE OF CONTENTS

INTRODUCTION

Obtain and maintain lean numbers, manage blood sugar levels, controlling nerve pain, and preventing dental problems are just a few reasons why many days are looking for ways to remove sugar from their diet. Although controlling one's sweet teeth can be one of the most frightening tasks even the tightest face diet, weight loss is very effective. There are many advantages to a sugar-free diet; However, why is it so difficult to stay away from sugar?

Many of us grow by enjoying classic desserts ranging from milk and cakes to apple pies. The cake accompanies many of the most significant lives. It is as if sugar-based food is a staple not only in our diets but also in our lives. Can anyone imagine a birthday party or marriage without mass flour, eggs, and fine processed sugar? Many frustrated diets feel that they cannot participate in celebrations if they do not participate in eating.

1. ROMAN ARTICHOKES

Artichokes look like big green flower buds. Not to be confused with Jerusalem artichokes, which are brown and resemble ginger root.

INGREDIENTS

- 2 cups fresh breadcrumbs, preferably whole-wheat bread
- One tablespoon of olive oil
- 4 large artichokes
- 2 lemons, halved
- 1/3 cup grated Parmesan cheese
- 3 garlic cloves, minced very small
- 2 tablespoons finely chopped flat-leaf (Italian) parsley
- 1 tablespoon grated lemon zest

- 1/4 teaspoon ground black pepper
- 1 cup and 2 to 4 tablespoons low sodium chicken or vegetable broth
- 1 cup of dry white wine
- 1 tablespoon minced shallots
- 1 teaspoon minced fresh oregano

NUTRITIONAL ANALYSIS PER SERVING

- Serving: 1/4 artichoke
- Calories123
- Total fat3 g
- Saturated fat1 g
- Trans fat Minimum amount
- Monounsaturated fat2 g
- Cholesterol3 mg
- Sodium179 mg
- Total carbohydrate18 g
- Dietary fiber5 g
- Total sugars2 g
- Added sugars0 g
- Protein6 g

2. BABA GANOUSH

Cooking vegetables on the grill helps to intensify the flavors. This recipe can be served hot or cold.

INGREDIENTS

- 1 head of garlic (about 8 cloves)
- 2 auberges, peeled and cut lengthwise
- 1 red bell pepper, halved and seeded
- Juice of 1 lemon (approximately 4 tablespoons)
- 1 tablespoon fresh basil, chopped
- 1 tablespoon of olive oil
- 1 teaspoon black pepper, or to taste
- 2 whole-grain Arabic loaves of bread or other flatbread

INSTRUCTIONS

Spray cold grill with cooking spray. Heat one side of the grill over high heat. (Or move the charcoal to the side of the grill.)

Cut off the top of the garlic bulb, wrap it in aluminum foil, and place it in the coldest part of the grill. Roast for 20 to 30 minutes. On the hot part of the grill, place the cut aubertites and the bell pepper. Grill for 2 to 3 minutes on each side.

Separate the roasted garlic from the bulb and place it in a food processor. Add the roasted eggplant and red pepper. Add the lemon juice, basil, olive oil, and pepper. Process until smooth. Scoop the sauce into a serving bowl.

Heat the bread on the grill for a few seconds on each side. Serve with the auberge paste.

NUTRITIONAL ANALYSIS PER SERVING

- Serving: One half of Arabic bread and 2 tablespoons of sauce
- Total carbohydrate40 g
- Dietary fiber12 g
- Sodium150 mg
- Saturated fat1 g
- Total fat5 g
- Trans fat0 g
- Cholesterol0 mg
- Protein7 g
- Monounsaturated fat2.5 g

- Calories233
- Added sugars0 g
- Total sugars11 g

3. TOMATO BRUSCHETTA WITH BASIL

For a drier topping, remove the seeds from the tomato before dicing it. (Cut the tomato in half and remove the seeds with your fingers or a spoon.)

INGREDIENTS

- 1/2 whole wheat bread baguette, cut into 6 diagonal 1/2-inch (1 cm) thick slices

- 2 tablespoons basil, chopped
- 1 tablespoon of chopped parsley
- 2 garlic cloves, minced
- 3 tomatoes, diced
- 1/2 cup fennel in cubes
- 1 teaspoon of olive oil
- 2 teaspoons balsamic vinegar
- 1 teaspoon black pepper

INSTRUCTIONS

Heat the oven to 400 ° F (200 ° C). Toast the baguette slices until lightly browned. Mix the rest of the ingredients. Spoon the mixture evenly over the toast. Serve immediately.

Nutritional analysis per serving

- Serving: 1 slice
- Total carbohydrate26 g
- Dietary fiber4 g
- Sodium123 mg
- Saturated fat Minimum amount
- Total fat2 g
- Trans fat0 g
- Cholesterol0 mg
- Protein5 g
- Monounsaturated fat<0.5 g
- Calories142
- Added sugars0 g
- Total sugars2 g

4. FRIED ROSTED BUTTERNUT SQUASH

To ensure even cooking, cut the vegetables into evenly sized pieces. This recipe can also be made with sweet potatoes or acorn squash.

INGREDIENTS

- 1 medium butternut squash
- 1 tablespoon of olive oil
- 1 tablespoon chopped fresh thyme
- 1 tablespoon minced fresh rosemary
- 1/2 teaspoon salt

INSTRUCTIONS

Heat the oven to 425 ° F (220 ° C). Lightly coat a cookie sheet with cooking spray.
Peel the butternut squash and cut it into even strips 1/2 inch (1 cm) wide by 3 inches (7.5 cm) long. In a medium bowl, mix the squash, oil, thyme, rosemary, and salt until the squash is well coated.

Distribute the pumpkin on the baking sheet and roast for 10 minutes. Remove the tray from the oven and shake it to separate the pumpkin strips. Return them to the oven and continue roasting for an additional 5 to 10 minutes until golden brown.

Nutritional analysis per serving

- Serving: 1/2 cup
- Calories62
- Total fat2 g
- Saturated fat0 g
- Trans fat0 g
- Monounsaturated fat2 g
- Cholesterol0 mg
- Sodium168 mg
- Total carbohydrate11 g
- Dietary fiber3 g
- Total sugars2 g
- Protein1 g

5. COCONUT SHRIMP

You can use smaller shrimp. Just keep in mind a smaller amount of breading and less cooking time.

INGREDIENTS

- 1/4 of Cup of sugared coconut
- 1/4 of Cup of panko breadcrumbs
- 1/2 teaspoon kosher salt
- 1/2 cup of coconut milk
- 12 large shrimp, peeled and deveined

INSTRUCTIONS

Heat the oven to 375 ° F (190 ° C). Lightly spray a cookie sheet with cooking spray.

Place the coconut, panko, and salt in a food processor and process until the mixture is uniform. Place the panko mixture in a small bowl. Place the coconut milk in another small bowl.

Dip each shrimp in the coconut milk, then panko mixture, and place on a cookie sheet. Lightly coat the tops of the shrimp with cooking spray. Bake until golden brown, 10-15 minutes.

NUTRITIONAL ANALYSIS PER SERVING

- Serving: 2 shrimp
- Calories75
- Total fat4 g
- Saturated fat2 g
- Trans fat0 g
- Monounsaturated fat2 g
- Cholesterol48 mg
- Sodium396 mg
- Total carbohydrate4 g
- Dietary fiber0 g
- Total sugars2 g
- Protein5 g

6. SHRIMP MARINATED IN LIME JUICE AND DIJON MUSTARD

In this recipe, the shrimp is marinated rather than served with a heavy sauce. Serve chilled with Melba crackers or toast.

INGREDIENTS

- 1 medium red onion, minced
- 1/2 cup fresh lime juice, plus lime zest for garnish
- 2 tablespoons capers
- 1 tablespoon Dijon mustard
- 1/2 teaspoon hot sauce
- 1 cup of water

- 1/2 cup of rice vinegar
- 3 whole cloves
- 1 bay leaf
- 1 pound (450g) uncooked shrimp, peeled and deveined (about 24 shrimp)

INSTRUCTIONS

In a shallow baking dish, combine the onion, lime juice, capers, mustard, and hot sauce. Reservation.
In a large saucepan, add the water, vinegar, cloves, and bay leaf. Bring it to a boil and add the shrimp. Cook for 1 minute, stirring constantly. Drain and transfer the shrimp to the shallow baking dish containing the onion mixture. Make sure to discard the cloves and bay leaf.

Stir to integrate the ingredients. Cover and refrigerate until chilled, about 1 hour.
To serve, divide the shrimp mixture into small individual bowls and garnish each with lime zest. Serve cold.

NUTRITIONAL ANALYSIS PER SERVING

- Portion: About 3 shrimp
- Calories60
- Total at minimum amount
- Saturated fat Minimum amount
- Trans fat Minimum amount
- Monounsaturated fat Minimum amount
- Cholesterol91 mg

7. SPICY CHIPOTLE SHRIMP

Shrimp are cooked when the meat turns opaque and white.

INGREDIENTS

- 1 pound (454 g) raw shrimp, peeled and deveined
- 2 tablespoons tomato paste
- 1 1/2 teaspoons of water
- 1/2 teaspoon of extra virgin olive oil
- 1/2 teaspoon minced garlic
- 1/2 teaspoon of chipotle chili powder
- 1/2 teaspoon fresh oregano, minced

INSTRUCTIONS

Rinse the shrimp in cold water. Pat dry with a paper towel and reserve on a plate.
In a small bowl, to make the marinade, whisk together the tomato paste, water, and oil. Add the garlic, chili powder, and oregano. Mix well.

Using a brush, spread the marinade (which will be thick) on both sides of the shrimp. Place in the refrigerator.
Build a fire in a charcoal grill or heat a gas grill or rotisserie. Away from a heat source, lightly coat the grill or grill with cooking spray. Place the cooking grate 4 to 6 inches (10 to 15 cm) from the heat source.

Put the shrimp in a grill basket or on skewers and place on the grill. Flip the shrimp after 3 to 4 minutes. Cooking time varies depending on the heat of the fire, so watch carefully.
Transfer to a plate and serve immediately.

NUTRITIONAL ANALYSIS PER SERVING

- Serving: 1/4 of the recipe
- Cholesterol182 mg
- Calories109
- Sodium139 mg
- Total fat1 g
- Total carbohydrate2 g
- Saturated fat Minimum amount
- Dietary fiber0.5 g
- Trans fat Minimum amount
- Added sugars0 g

- Monounsaturated fat0.5 g
- Protein23 g
- Total sugars0 g

8. CRISPY POTATO SKINS

You can use any herb or spice to season the potato skins. Try fresh basil, chives, dill, garlic, cayenne pepper, caraway seed, tarragon, or thyme.

INGREDIENTS

- 2 medium Russet potatoes
- Butter flavored cooking spray
- 1 tablespoon minced fresh rosemary
- 1/8 teaspoon freshly ground black pepper

INSTRUCTIONS

Heat the oven to 375 ° F (190 ° C).
Wash the potatoes and pierce them with a fork. Place in the oven and cook until the skins are crisp about 1 hour.

Carefully – the potatoes will be very hot – cut them in half and remove the pulp, leaving about 1/8 inch (3 mm) of the potato pulp adhering to the skin. Save the pulp for another use.

Spray the inside of the skin of each potato with butter-flavored cooking spray. Press the rosemary and pepper. Put the skins back in the oven for 5 to 10 minutes. Serve immediately.

NUTRITIONAL ANALYSIS PER SERVING

- Portion: 2 pieces
- Total at minimum amount
- Calories fifty
- Protein2 g
- Cholesterol0 mg
- Total carbohydrate10 g
- Dietary fiber4 g
- Monounsaturated fat Minimum amount
- Saturated fat Minimum amount
- Trans fat0 g
- Sodium12 mg
- Added sugars0 g
- Total sugars1 g

9. SOUTHWESTERN-STYLE POTATO SKINS

These potato skins are a very good source of iron, B vitamins, and fiber.

INGREDIENTS

- 6 large baking potatoes
- 1 teaspoon of olive oil
- 1 teaspoon chili powder
- 1/8 teaspoon chili sauce

- 6 slices turkey bacon, cooked until crisp, chopped
- 1 medium tomato, diced
- 2 tablespoons sliced green onions (chives)
- 1/2 cup cheddar cheese shredded

INSTRUCTIONS

Heat the oven to 450 ° F (230 ° C). Lightly spray a cookie sheet with cooking spray.
Scrub the potatoes and prick each one several times with a fork. Microwave uncovered on full power until tender, about 10 minutes. Remove the potatoes from the microwave and place them on a wire rack to cool.

When cool to the touch, cut each potato in half lengthwise and scoop out the pulp with a spoon. Leave about 1/4 inch (0.5 cm) of the pulp attached to the rind. (Save the pulp of the potatoes for another meal.)

In a small bowl, whisk together the olive oil, chili powder, and hot sauce. Spread the olive oil mixture on the inside of the potato skins. Cut each half of the potato skin in half again crosswise. Place the potatoes on the cookie sheet.

In a small bowl, gently mix the turkey bacon, tomato, and onions. Fill each potato peel with this mixture and sprinkle each with cheese.
Bake for about 10 minutes until the cheese is melted and the potato skins are hot. Serve immediately.

NUTRITIONAL ANALYSIS PER SERVING

- Serving: 2 shells
- Calories194
- Total fat6 g
- Saturated fat3 g
- Trans fat0 g
- Monounsaturated fat2 g

- Cholesterol20 mg
- Sodium164 mg
- Total carbohydrate27 g
- Dietary fiber6 g
- Total sugars2 g
- Added sugars0 g
- Protein8 g

10. SHRIMP CEVICHE

The term "ceviche" refers to both a technique and a typical dish from Central and South America. Raw fish or shellfish is cooked (cured) without heat in acidic citrus juices, and seasoned with various herbs and spices.

INGREDIENTS

- 1/2-pound (225g) raw shellfish, cut into 1/4-inch (0.5cm) pieces
- 2 lemons, zest and juice
- 2 limes, zest, and juice
- 2 tablespoons olive oil

- 2 teaspoons cumin
- 1/2 cup of red onion cut into cubes
- 1 cup diced tomatoes
- 2 tablespoons minced garlic
- 1 cup black beans, cooked
- 1/4 of Cup of serrano peppers cut into cubes and without seeds
- 1 cup cucumber cut into cubes, peeled, and seeded
- 1/4 of Cup of coriander chopped

INSTRUCTIONS

Place shrimp in a shallow skillet and top with lemon and lime juice; reserve the zest. Refrigerate for at least 3 hours or until shrimp are firm and white.
Mix the remaining ingredients in a separate bowl and set aside while the shrimp cook cold.

When you're ready to serve, mix the shrimp and citrus juice with the remaining ingredients. Serve with baked nachos.

NUTRITIONAL ANALYSIS PER SERVING

- Serving: About 3/4 cup
- Calories98
- Total fat4 g
- Saturated fat1 g
- Trans fat Minimum amount
- Monounsaturated fat3 g
- Cholesterol36 mg
- Sodium167 mg
- Total carbohydrate10 g
- Dietary fiber3 g
- Added sugars0 g
- Protein7 g

11. ROASTED PORTOBELLO MUSHROOMS MARINATED WITH GINGER

Portobello mushrooms are firm in texture and have virtually no fat or sodium.

INGREDIENTS

- 1/4 cup balsamic vinegar
- 1/2 cup of pineapple juice
- 2 tablespoons minced fresh ginger, peeled
- 4 large portobello mushrooms (about 4 ounces or 113 g each), clean and stemmed
- 1 tablespoon fresh basil, chopped

INSTRUCTIONS

In a small bowl, whisk together the balsamic vinegar, pineapple juice, and ginger.
Place the mushrooms in a glass dish, stemless side up. Spread the marinade over the mushrooms. Cover and marinate in the refrigerator for about 1 hour, turning the mushrooms once.

Build a fire in a charcoal grill or heat a gas grill or rotisserie. Away from the heat source, lightly coat grill or grill with cooking spray. Place the cooking grate 4 to 6 inches (10 to 15 cm) from the heat source.

Grill mushrooms over medium heat, frequently stirring, for about 5 minutes on each side, until tender. Brush with the marinade to prevent them from drying out.
Using tongs, transfer the mushrooms to the serving dish. Garnish with basil and serve immediately.

NUTRITIONAL ANALYSIS PER SERVING

- Serving: 1 mushroom
- Cholesterol0 mg
- Calories60
- Sodium15 mg
- Total at minimum amount
- Total carbohydrate12 g
- Saturated fat Minimum amount
- Dietary fiber2 g
- Trans fat0 g
- Added sugars0 g
- Monounsaturated fat Minimum amount
- Protein3 g

- Total sugars8 g

12. PORTOBELLO MUSHROOMS MARINATED WITH PROVOLONE

When cleaning mushrooms, do not submerge them in water because they will absorb water like a sponge. Instead, clean the mushrooms with a damp cloth or heavy paper towel.

INGREDIENTS

- 2 portobello mushrooms, stemmed and cleaned
- 1/2 cup balsamic vinegar
- 1 tablespoon brown sugar
- 1/4 teaspoon dehydrated rosemary
- 1 teaspoon minced garlic
- 1/4 cup (1 ounce [30 g]) provolone cheese, grate

Instructions

Heat the broiler pan. Place the grill 4 inches (10 cm) away from the heat source. Lightly spray a glass baking dish with cooking spray. Place the mushrooms in the pan, stem (gill) cut side up.

In a small bowl, whisk together the vinegar, brown sugar, rosemary, and garlic. Pour the mixture over the mushrooms. Set aside for 5 to 10 minutes to marinate.

Grill (grill) the mushrooms, turning once, until tender, about 4 minutes on each side. Sprinkle grated cheese over each mushroom and continue to grill (grill) until cheese is melted. Place on individual plates.

Nutritional analysis per serving

- Serving: 1 mushroom
- Calories112
- Total fat4 g
- Saturated fat2 g
- Trans fat Minimum amount
- Monounsaturated fat1 g
- Cholesterol10 mg
- Sodium140 mg
- Total carbohydrate13 g
- Dietary fiber1 g
- Total sugars11 g
- Added sugars4 g
- Protein6 g

13. MUSHROOMS STUFFED WITH BASIL PESTO

This appetizer can be made ahead of time. Refrigerate until serving time.

INGREDIENTS

- Ingredients for the topping:
- 1 1/2 cup panko breadcrumbs
- 1/4 of Cup of butter, melted
- 3 tablespoons minced fresh parsley
- Filling:
- 2 cups fresh basil leaves
- 1/4 of Cup of fresh Parmesan cheese
- 2 tablespoons pumpkin seeds

- 1 tablespoon of olive oil
- 1 tablespoon fresh garlic
- 2 teaspoons lemon juice
- 1/2 teaspoon kosher salt

INSTRUCTIONS

Heat the oven to 350 ° F (175 ° C). Place the mushroom hats upside down on a cookie sheet.

To prepare the topping, in a small bowl, combine the panko breadcrumbs, butter, and parsley; reservation.

To prepare the filling, place the basil, cheese, pumpkin seeds, oil, garlic, lemon juice, and salt in a food processor. Process until evenly mixed.

Generously fill the mushroom hats with the basil pesto filling. Sprinkle each mushroom with about 1 teaspoon of the panko coating. Press the cover gently with your hand. Bake for 10 to 15 minutes or until golden brown.

NUTRITIONAL ANALYSIS PER SERVING

- Serving: 1 mushroom
- Calories59
- Total fat3 g
- Saturated fat2 g
- Trans fat0 g
- Monounsaturated fat1 g
- Cholesterol7 mg
- Sodium80 mg
- Total carbohydrate4 g
- Dietary fiber0 g
- Total sugars0 g

- Protein2 g

14. FRESH TOMATO CROSTINI

Crostini, in Italian, means "small toast." These small toasts are topped with a tomato, basil, and garlic mixture.

INGREDIENTS

- 4 Roma tomatoes, chopped
- 1/4 of Cup of fresh basil chopped
- 2 teaspoons olive oil
- 1 clove garlic, minced
- Freshly ground pepper
- 1/4 pound (115g) crisp Italian peasant bread, cut into 4 slices and toasted

INSTRUCTIONS

Combine the tomatoes, basil, oil, garlic, and pepper in a medium bowl. Cover and let stand 30 minutes. Cover the toasts using the tomato mixture with any of the juices. Serve at room temperature.

Nutritional analysis per serving

- Serving: 1 slice
- Calories107
- Total fat3.5 g
- Saturated fat0.6 g
- Trans fat0 g
- Monounsaturated fat2 g
- Cholesterol0 mg
- Sodium176 mg
- Total carbohydrate16 g
- Dietary fiber1 g
- Added sugars0 g
- Protein3 g

15. BAKED BRIE CHEESE WRAPS

Make this appetizer the day before your guests arrive. Store covered in the refrigerator until ready to bake.

INGREDIENTS

- 1/2 cup fresh or frozen cranberries
- 1/2 medium orange, quartered
- 2 tablespoons sugar
- 1 cinnamon stick
- 1 sheet of puff pastry, cut into 12 1/4 oz (7g) squares
- 6 ounces (170g) brie cheese, cut into 1/2-ounce (14g) cubes
- 2 tablespoons of water
- 1 egg whit

INSTRUCTIONS

Heat the oven to 425 ° F (220 ° C).

Heat small skillet over medium-high heat; lightly spray with cooking spray. Reduce to low heat. Place the cranberries, orange, sugar and cinnamon stick in the skillet and cook for about 10 minutes; Stir constantly until cranberries are soft and mixture begins to thicken. Remove from the fire and let cool. Remove the cinnamon stick and the orange pieces.

Roll out each square of puff pastry. Place a cube of cheese and 1 teaspoon of the cooled cranberry mixture on each square of puff pastry. In a small bowl, mix the water and the egg white. Using a pastry brush, apply a small amount of egg mixture to the inside of the puff pastry.

Pull one end of the puff pastry at a time around the cheese and cranberry mixture as a wrap. Spread the top of the dough with the egg mixture. Place the wrapped ones on a cookie sheet and bake for 10 to 12 minutes or until golden brown.

Nutritional analysis per serving

- Serving: 1 wrapped
- Calories116
- Total fat7 g
- Saturated fat4 g
- Trans fat0 g
- Monounsaturated fat2 g
- Cholesterol22 mg
- Sodium133 mg

- Total carbohydrate9 g
- Dietary fiber0 g
- Total sugars4 g
- Protein4 g

16. PICKLED ASPARAGUS

To ensure safe consumption, sterilize the jars and lids by immersing them in boiling water for 5 minutes. Let them cool to room temperature before filling them.

INGREDIENTS

- 1 pound (450g) fresh asparagus, stems removed (about 3 cups)
- 1/4 cup pearl onions
- 1/4 cup of white wine vinegar
- 1/4 of Cup of cider vinegar
- 1 sprig of fresh dill (or 2 teaspoons of dried dill)
- 1 cup of water
- 2 whole cloves
- 3 garlic cloves, whole

- 8 whole peppercorns
- 1/4 of teaspoon of red pepper flakes
- 6 whole coriander seeds

INSTRUCTIONS

Trim the woody ends of the asparagus and cut the stems to lengths suitable for the jars. Place the stems in a colander, wash well, and drain. Trim the onions. Combine all ingredients in airtight containers. Keep in the refrigerator for up to 4 weeks.

NUTRITIONAL ANALYSIS PER SERVING

- Serving: 1/2 cup
- Total carbohydrate4 g
- Dietary fiber2 g
- Sodium5 mg
- Saturated fat Minimum amount
- Total fat Minimum amount
- Trans fat0 g
- Cholesterol0 mg
- Protein2 g
- Monounsaturated fat Minimum amount
- Calories24
- Added sugars0 mg
- Total sugars2 g

17. ROASTED RED PEPPER HUMMUS

Store the hummus in the refrigerator for up to a week. Use as a spread on burritos or sandwiches.

INGREDIENTS

- 2 cups chickpeas
- 1 cup roasted red bell pepper, sliced and seeded
- 2 tablespoons white sesame seeds
- 1 tablespoon of lemon juice
- 1 tablespoon of olive oil
- 1 1/4 teaspoon cumin
- 1 teaspoon onion powder
- 1 teaspoon garlic powder
- 1 teaspoon kosher salt
- 1/4 teaspoon cayenne pepper

INSTRUCTIONS

In a food processor, mix all ingredients until smooth.

NUTRITIONAL ANALYSIS PER SERVING

- Serving: 3 tablespoons
- Calories53
- Total fat2 g
- Saturated fat0 g
- Trans fat0 g
- Monounsaturated fat1 g
- Cholesterol0 mg
- Sodium126 mg
- Total carbohydrate7 g
- Dietary fiber2 g
- Total sugars1 g
- Protein2 g

18. PEANUT BUTTER HUMMUS

This fresh version of traditional hummus can be spread on sandwiches or served as a dip to accompany apples and celery.

INGREDIENTS

- 2 cups chickpeas
- 1 cup of water
- 1/2 cup powdered peanut butter
- 1/4 of Cup of natural peanut butter
- 2 tablespoons brown sugar
- 1 teaspoon vanilla extract

INSTRUCTIONS

Place all the ingredients in a food processor. Process until smooth. Refrigerate for up to 1 week.

NUTRITIONAL ANALYSIS PER SERVING

- Serving: 2 tablespoons
- Calories135
- Total fat4 g
- Saturated fat0 g
- Trans fat0 g
- Monounsaturated fat1 g
- Cholesterol0 mg
- Sodium47 mg
- Total carbohydrate19 g
- Dietary fiber4 g
- Total sugars4 g
- Protein7 g

19. GLUTEN-FREE HUMMUS

In this recipe, the tahini, which sometimes contains gluten, is replaced by olive oil. Sherry vinegar is also used instead of lemon juice.

INGREDIENTS

- 2/3 cup chickpeas, selected and rinsed, soaked in water overnight and drained
- 3 cups of water
- 2 cloves of garlic
- 1 bay leaf
- 1/2 teaspoon salt
- 1 tablespoon of olive oil
- 3/4 cup plus 2 tablespoons sliced green onions (scallions)
- 2 tablespoons sherry vinegar
- 3 tablespoons chopped fresh coriander (coriander)
- 1 teaspoon ground cumin

INSTRUCTIONS

In a large saucepan over high heat, combine the chickpeas, water, garlic cloves, bay leaf, and 1/4 teaspoon of salt. Bring the pot to a boil. Reduce heat to low, cover partially, and simmer for 50 to 60 minutes, until chickpeas are tender. Drain and discard the bay leaf, reserving the garlic and 1/2 cup of the cooking liquid.

In a blender or food processor, combine the chickpeas, cooked garlic, olive oil, 3/4 cup green onion, vinegar, cilantro, cumin, and the remaining 1/4 teaspoon salt. Process to puree. Add reserved cooking liquid, 1 tablespoon at a time, until mixture is thick.

In a serving bowl, stir the chickpea mixture and the other 2 tablespoons green onion. Serve immediately or cover and store in the refrigerator until ready to use. Makes about 1 1/2 cup.

NUTRITIONAL ANALYSIS PER SERVING

- Serving: 1/4 cup
- Total carbohydrate15 g
- Dietary fiber4 g
- Sodium210 mg
- Saturated fat0.5 g
- Total fat4 g
- Cholesterol0 mg
- Protein5 g
- Monounsaturated fat2 g
- Calories116
- Trans fat0 g

- Total sugars3 g
- Added sugars0 g

20. HUMUS

For a different flavor, you can substitute the chickpeas for white beans, butter beans, or lima beans and the paprika for 1 teaspoon of toasted and ground cumin seeds.

INGREDIENTS

- 2 cans (16 oz [450 g] each) reduced sodium chickpeas, rinsed and drained except 1/4 cup liquid
- 1 tablespoon of extra virgin olive oil
- 1/4 of Cup of yellow lemon juice
- 2 garlic cloves, minced
- 1/4 of teaspoon of black pepper, crushed

- 1/4 of teaspoon of paprika
- 3 tablespoons tahini (sesame paste) *
- 2 tablespoons flat-leaf Italian parsley

Note: If you need to follow a gluten-free diet, check the label to make sure the brand of tahini is gluten-free.

INSTRUCTIONS

Using a blender or food processor, puree the chickpeas. Add the olive oil, lemon juice, garlic, pepper, paprika, tahini, and parsley. Blend well.

Add the reserved liquid, 1 tablespoon at a time, until the mixture has the consistency of a thick paste.

Serve immediately or cover and store in the refrigerator until ready to use.

NUTRITIONAL ANALYSIS PER SERVING

- Serving: 1/4 cup
- Calories88
- Total fat4 g
- Saturated fat<1 g
- Trans fat0 g
- Monounsaturated fat2 g
- Cholesterol0 mg
- Sodium80 mg
- Total carbohydrate9 g
- Dietary fiber3 g
- Total sugars2 g
- Added sugars0 g
- Protein4 g

21. FRESH FUIRT KEBABS

These skewers go well with any type of fruit, even more of the exotic type such as star fruit, dwarf orange, or prickly pear. To prevent the fruit from turning dark, dip it in pineapple or orange juice.

INGREDIENTS

- 6 ounces (170g) low-fat unsweetened lemon yogurt
- 1 teaspoon fresh lime juice
- 1 teaspoon lime zest
- 4 pineapple chunks (about 1/2 inch [1 cm] each)
- 4 strawberries
- 1 kiwi, peeled and cut into quarters
- 1/2 banana, cut into 4 1/2-inch (1 cm) pieces
- 4 red grapes
- 4 wooden skewers

INSTRUCTIONS

In a small bowl, combine the yogurt, lime juice, and lime zest. Cover and refrigerate until needed.
Place 1 fruit of each variety on the skewer. Repeat the process with the rest of the skewers until no fruit remains. Serve with the lemon-lime sauce.

NUTRITIONAL ANALYSIS PER SERVING

- Serving: 2 fruit kebabs
- Calories190
- Total fat2 g
- Saturated fat1 g
- Trans fat0 g
- Monounsaturated fat Minimum amount
- Cholesterol5 mg
- Sodium53 mg
- Total carbohydrate39 mg
- Dietary fiber4 g
- Added sugars6 g
- Protein4 g

22. SWEET AND SPICY SNACK MIX

Instead of peanuts and pretzels, this snack mix contains chickpeas and dried fruit. With this spicy snack mix, you not only increase the amount of fiber, but you also reduce the fat and sodium content.

INGREDIENTS

- 2 cans (15 oz. [425 g] each) chickpeas, rinsed, drained, and dried
- 2 cups of wheat cereal in squares
- 1 cup of dehydrated pineapple chunks
- 1 cup raisins
- 2 tablespoons of honey
- 2 tablespoons Worcestershire sauce

- 1 teaspoon garlic powder
- 1/2 teaspoon chili powder

INSTRUCTIONS

Heat the oven to 350 ° F (175 ° C). Lightly spray a 15 1/2 × 10 1/2-inch (40 × 25 cm) cookie sheet with butter-flavored cooking spray.

Spray a heavy skillet with plenty of butter-flavored cooking spray. Add the chickpeas to the skillet and cook over medium heat for about 10 minutes, stirring frequently, until the chickpeas begin to brown. Transfer the chickpeas to the prepared cookie sheet. Spray them lightly with cooking spray. Bake for about 20 minutes, stirring frequently, until the chickpeas are crisp.

Lightly coat a baking dish with butter-flavored cooking spray. Add the cereal, pineapple, and raisins to the skillet. Add the roasted chickpeas. Stir to mix well.
In a large glass measuring cup, combine the honey, Worcestershire sauce, and spices. Stir to mix well. Pour the mixture over the snack mix and stir slowly. Re-spray the mixture with cooking spray. Bake for 10 to 15 minutes, stirring a few times to avoid burning the mixture.
Remove from the oven and let it cool. Store in an airtight container.

NUTRITIONAL ANALYSIS PER SERVING

- Serving: 1/2 cup
- Total fat2 g
- Calories194
- Protein5 g
- Cholesterol0 mg
- Total carbohydrate39 g

- Dietary fiber5 g
- Monounsaturated fat0.5 g
- Saturated fat Minimum amount
- Added sugars3 g
- Sodium218 mg
- Trans fat0 g

23. ROASTED POTATOES WITH GARLIC AND HERBS

Potatoes are a good source of vitamin C, vitamin B6, and potassium. If eaten with the skin, the amount of fiber almost doubles.

INGREDIENTS

- 3/4 pound (340 g) small (2-inch [5 cm]) white or red potatoes
- 4 cloves of garlic
- 2 teaspoons olive oil
- 2 teaspoons minced fresh rosemary
- 1/8 teaspoon of salt
- 1/4 of teaspoon of ground black pepper
- 2 teaspoons of butter
- 2 tablespoons minced fresh parsley

INSTRUCTIONS

Heat the oven to 400 ° F (200 ° C). Lightly spray a large baking dish with cooking spray.

In a large bowl, add the whole potatoes, garlic cloves, olive oil, rosemary, salt, and pepper. Mix well (with your hands is best) until the potatoes are evenly coated with the oil and spices.

Place a single layer of potatoes in the prepared baking dish. Cover with a lid or foil and bake for 25 minutes.

Remove the lid or foil. Flip the potatoes and bake, uncovered, until soft and lightly browned, about 25 minutes.

Transfer them to a serving bowl and mix them with the butter. Sprinkle with parsley and serve.

Nutritional analysis per serving

- Serving: 2/3 cup approximately
- Total carbohydrate15 g
- Dietary fiber2 g
- Sodium103 mg
- Saturated fat2 g
- Total fat4 g
- Trans fat Minimum amount
- Cholesterol5 mg
- Protein2 g
- Monounsaturated fat2 g
- Calories104
- Added sugars0 g
- Total sugars1 g

24. SMOKE TROUT PASTA

This easy-to-make spread can be made up to a week in advance and stored tightly covered in the refrigerator. Serve on whole grain crackers or thinly toasted baguette slices.

INGREDIENTS

- 1/4 pound (115 g) smoked trout fillets, skinned and cut into pieces
- 1/2 cup 1 percent low-fat cottage cheese
- 1/4 cup red onion, coarsely chopped
- 2 teaspoons fresh lemon juice
- 1 teaspoon hot chili sauce
- 1/2 teaspoon Worcestershire sauce
- 1 stalk celery, diced

INSTRUCTIONS

In a blender or food processor, combine the trout, cottage cheese, red onion, lemon juice, hot pepper sauce, and Worcestershire sauce. Process until smooth; Interrupt the process to scrape down the sides of the bowl as needed. Add the diced celery. Cover and refrigerate until before serving.

NUTRITIONAL ANALYSIS PER SERVING

Serving: 1 tablespoon
Calories29
Total fat1 g
Saturated fat Minimum amount
Trans fat0 g
Monounsaturated fat0.5 mg
Cholesterol7 mg
Sodium87 mg
Total carbohydrate1 g
Dietary fiber Minimum amount
Total sugars Minimum amount
Added sugars0 g
Protein4 g

25. ROASTED PINEAPPLE

This Caribbean-style marinade and the heat of the grill add a smoky sweetness to this pineapple dessert.

INGREDIENTS

For the marinade

- 2 tablespoons dark honey
- 1 tablespoon of olive oil
- 1 tablespoon fresh lime juice
- 1 teaspoon ground cinnamon
- 1/4 of teaspoon of ground cloves
- 1 firm pineapple, ripe
- 8 wooden skewers, soaked in water for 30 minutes, or metal skewers

- 1 tablespoon golden rum (optional)
- 1 tablespoon lime zest

INSTRUCTIONS

Build a fire on a charcoal grill or heat your gas grill or broiler. Away from heat, lightly spray grill or broiler pan with cooking spray. Place the grill 4 to 6 inches (10 to 15 cm) from the heat source.

To prepare the marinade, in a small bowl, add the honey, olive oil, lime juice, cinnamon, and cloves, and mix well. Reservation.

Cut the crown of leaves and the base of the pineapple. Stand the pineapple upright and cut the skin with a large sharp knife, down, just below the surface, into long vertical strips, but leave the small brown "eyes" of the fruit. Lay the pineapple on its side.

Align the blade of the knife with the diagonal rows of the eyes and cut a shallow groove, following a spiral pattern around the pineapple to remove all the eyes. Stand the pineapple upright and cut it in half, lengthwise.

Place each pineapple half cut side down and cut lengthwise into four large wedges; cut the center. Cut each segment crosswise into three pieces. Place three pieces of pineapple on each skewer.

Lightly brush the pineapple with the marinade. Grill the pineapple or grill it for about 5 minutes on each side; flip once and brush once or twice with the remaining marinade until tender and golden.

Remove the pineapple from the skewers and place on a platter or individual plates. Brush with rum, if desired, and drizzle with lime zest. You can serve it hot or warm.

NUTRITIONAL ANALYSIS PER SERVING

- Portion: 1/8 pineapple and marinade
- Total carbohydrate13 g
- Dietary fiber1 g
- Sodium1 mg
- Saturated fat<1 g
- Total fat2 g
- Cholesterol0 mg
- Protein<1 g
- Monounsaturated fat1 g
- Calories70
- Added sugars0 g
- Trans fat0 g

26. ADVOCADO SALSA

Avocado is high in monounsaturated fat and is a great source of lutein, an antioxidant that can protect vision.

INGREDIENTS

1/2 cup fat-free sour cream
2 teaspoons chopped onion
1/8 teaspoon hot sauce
1 ripe avocado, peeled, pitted, and mashed (about 1/2 cup)
Instructions
In a small bowl, place the sour cream, onion, hot sauce, and avocado. Mix the ingredients evenly. Serve with baked nachos or sliced vegetables.

NUTRITIONAL ANALYSIS PER SERVING

Serving: 1/4 cup
Total carbohydrate8 g
Dietary fiber2.5 g
Sodium57 mg
Saturated fat1 g
Total fat5 g
Trans fat0 g
Cholesterol3 mg
Protein2 g
Monounsaturated fat3 g
Calories85
Added sugars0 g
Total sugars Minimum amount

27. WHITE BEAN SAUCE

To cook garlic in the oven, cut the branches off several garlic heads, exposing the cloves. Spray the garlic generously with cooking spray. Wrap in foil also sprayed with cooking spray. Heat the oven to 350 ° F (175 ° C) and cook for 30 minutes.

INGREDIENTS

- 1 15-ounce (425g) can white kidney beans (cannellini), rinsed and drained
- 8 garlic cloves, baked
- 2 tablespoons olive oil
- 2 tablespoons lemon juice

INSTRUCTIONS

In a blender or food processor, place the beans, baked garlic, olive oil, and lemon juice. Blend until smooth. Serve on thin slices of toasted French bread or pita bread triangles. Also, great when placed on top of squared red (sweet) bell peppers.

NUTRITIONAL ANALYSIS PER SERVING

- Serving: 2 tablespoons
- Calories84
- Total fat4 g
- Saturated fat0.5 g
- Trans fat0 g
- Monounsaturated fat2 g
- Cholesterol0 mg
- Sodium123 mg
- Total carbohydrate9 g
- Dietary fiber3 g
- Added sugars0 g
- Protein3 g

28. FRUIT SAUCE WITH SWEET NACHOS

This kid-friendly recipe is easy, and can be made by young cooks with little help from adults.

Ingredients

- For the crispy tortillas:

- 8 whole wheat and fat free tortillas
- Cooking spray
- 1 spoon of sugar
- 1/2 tablespoon of cinnamon
- For the fruit sauce:
- 3 cups of diced fresh fruit, such as apples, oranges, kiwi, strawberries, grapes, or other fresh fruit
- 2 tablespoons of unsweetened jam, any flavor
- 1 tablespoon honey or agave nectar
- 2 tablespoons orange juice

INSTRUCTIONS

Preheat the oven to 350 ° F (175 ° C). Cut each tortilla into 8 triangular pieces. Place the pieces on two baking sheets. Make sure they don't overlap. Spray the tortilla pieces with cooking spray.

In a small bowl, add the water and cinnamon. Sprinkle evenly over tortilla pieces. Bake 10 to 12 minutes or until chunks are crisp. Place them on a wire rack and let them cool.

Cut the fruits into cubes. Gently mix the fruits in a bowl. In another bowl, whisk together the jam, honey and orange juice. Pour this mixture over the cubed fruit. Mix gently. Cover the bowl with plastic wrap and refrigerate for 2 to 3 hours.

Serve as a dip or on top of the cinnamon nachos.

NUTRITIONAL ANALYSIS PER SERVING

Serving Size: About 8 nachos and 1/3 cup salsa
Total carbohydrate24 g
Dietary fiber10 g
Sodium181 mg
Saturated fat Minimum amount
Total fat Minimum amount
Trans fat Minimum amount
Cholesterol0 mg
Protein2 g
Monounsaturated fat Minimum amount
Calories105
Total sugars8 g

Added sugars4 g

29. CORN AND BLACK BEAN SAUCE

For a spicier seasoning, substitute coriander for parsley, or add chili powder to your liking.

INGREDIENTS

- 1 can (15.5 ounces) black beans, rinsed and drained (about 2 cups)
- 1 cup frozen corn kernels, thawed at room temperature
- 4 tomatoes, seeded and diced (about 3 cups)
- 2 garlic cloves, minced
- 1/2 medium red onion, diced (about 1/2 cup)
- 1/2 cup of chopped parsley
- 1 green, yellow, or red bell pepper, seeded and diced (about 1 cup)
- 2 teaspoons sugar
- Juice of 1 lemon

INSTRUCTIONS

In a large bowl, mix all the ingredients. Stir gently to mix. Cover and refrigerate for at least 30 minutes to allow the flavors to combine.

NUTRITIONAL ANALYSIS PER SERVING

- Serving: 1 cup approximately
- Total fat0.5 g
- Calories112
- Protein5 g
- Cholesterol0 mg
- Total carbohydrate22 g
- Dietary fiber6 g
- Monounsaturated fat Minimum amount
- Saturated fat Minimum amount
- Trans fat0 g
- Sodium93 mg
- Total sugars3 g
- Added sugars1 g

30. WATERMELON AND CRANBERRY FRESH WATER

Agues Frescas are popular fresh fruit drinks in Mexico. While water is a standard ingredient, this undiluted version is good for quenching your thirst.

INGREDIENTS

- 2 1/2 pounds (1.15 kg) watermelon, seeded, peeled and diced (about 7 cups)
- 1 cup fructose cranberry juice (sometimes called cranberry nectar)
- 1/4 cup fresh lime juice
- 1 lime cut into 6 slices

Instructions

Place the watermelon in a blender or food processor. Process until smooth. Pass the puree through a fine mesh sieve placed over a bowl to remove the pulp and clarify the juice. Pour the juice into a large pitcher. Add the cranberry and lime juices and stir to combine.

Refrigerate until cool. Pour into chilled tall glasses and garnish each with a lime wedge.

NUTRITIONAL ANALYSIS PER SERVING

- Serving: About 3/4 cup
- Total carbohydrate20 g
- Dietary fiber1 g
- Sodium9 mg
- Saturated fat0 g
- Total fat0 g
- Cholesterol0 mg
- Protein1 g
- Monounsaturated fat0 g
- Calories84
- Trans fat0 g
- Total sugars16 g
- Added sugars0 g

31. AMBROSIA WITH COCONUT AND TOASTED ALMONDS

This southern classic provides 45 milligrams of vitamin C, which is more than 75 percent of the recommended daily intake.

INGREDIENTS

- 1/2 cup of sliced almonds
- 1/2 cup unsweetened grated coconut
- 1 small pineapple, diced (about 3 cups)
- 5 oranges, cut into wedges
- 2 red apples, cored and diced
- 1 banana, peeled, cut lengthwise in half and sliced crosswise
- 2 tablespoons sherry wine Cream

- Fresh mint leaves for garnish

INSTRUCTIONS

Heat the oven to 325 ° F (160 ° C). Place the almonds on a cookie sheet and bake; Stir a few times until golden brown and fragrant, about 10 minutes. Immediately transfer to a plate to cool. Add the coconut to the pan and bake, stirring frequently, until lightly browned, about 10 minutes. Immediately transfer to a plate to cool.

In a large bowl, mix the pineapple, oranges, apples, banana, and sherry. Stir gently to mix well. Spoon the fruit mixture evenly into separate individual bowls. Sprinkle evenly with toasted almonds and coconut, and garnish with mint. Serve immediately.

NUTRITIONAL ANALYSIS PER SERVING

- Serving: 1 cup
- Calories177
- Total fat5 g
- Saturated fat1 g
- Trans fat Minimum amount
- Monounsaturated fat2 g
- Cholesterol0 mg
- Sodium2 mg
- Total carbohydrate30 g
- Dietary fiber6 g
- Total sugars21 g
- Added sugars0 g
- Protein3 g

32. SAUTEED BANANAS

Walnut oil adds an exotic accent, but you can substitute canola oil for it. Similarly, rum can be replaced with apple juice.

INGREDIENTS

For the sauce:

- 1 tablespoon butter
- 1 tablespoon of walnut oil
- 1 tablespoon of honey
- 2 tablespoons packed brown sugar
- 3 tablespoons 1 percent low-fat milk
- 1 tablespoon black raisins or golden raisins (sultanas))
- To fry:
- 4 firm consistency bananas, about 1 pound (450 g) total weight
- 1/2 teaspoon canola oil

- 2 tablespoons dark rum

INSTRUCTIONS

Start by making the sauce. In a small saucepan, melt the butter over low heat. Mix in the walnut oil, honey and brown sugar. Cook for about 3 minutes, stirring continuously, until the sugar dissolves.

Add the milk, 1 tablespoon at a time, then cook for about 3 minutes, stirring continuously, until the sauce thickens slightly. Remove from the heat and add the raisins. Reserve and keep warm.

Peel the bananas, and then cut each one crosswise into 3 pieces. Cut each piece in half lengthwise. Lightly spray a large nonstick skillet with canola oil and set over medium-high heat. Add the bananas and sauté for 3 to 4 minutes, until they start to brown. Transfer them to a plate, and keep them warm.

Add the rum to the skillet, bring to a boil and deglaze the pan; Stir with a wooden spoon to remove the browned parts from the bottom of the skillet. Cook for about 30 to 45 seconds until reduced by half. Put the bananas back in the pan to reheat.

To serve, divide the bananas into individual plates or bowls. Drizzle with the warm sauce and serve immediately.

NUTRITIONAL ANALYSIS PER SERVING

- Serving Size: 4 banana chunks and about 1 1/2 tablespoon salsa
- Total carbohydrate27 g

- Dietary fiber2 g
- Sodium21 mg
- Saturated fat2 g
- Total fat5 g
- Trans fat Minimum amount
- Cholesterol5 mg
- Protein1 g
- Monounsaturated fat1 g
- Calories145
- Added sugars8 g
- Total sugars18 g

33. NUT AND FRUIT BAR

When you want a treat, eat this healthy treat.

INGREDIENTS

- 1/2 cup quinoa flour
- 1/2 cup oatmeal
- 1/4 cup flaxseed meal
- 1/4 cup wheat germ
- 1/4 cup of chopped almonds
- 1/4 cup dried apricots, chopped (about 5 apricot halves)
- 1/4 cup minced dehydrated figs (about 5 figs)
- 1/4 cup honey
- 1/4 cup dehydrated pineapple, chopped
- 2 tablespoons cornstarch

INSTRUCTIONS

Line a baking sheet with parchment paper. Combine all the ingredients, and mix well. Press the mixture into the iron to a thickness of half an inch (1.30 cm). Bake at 300 ° F (150 ° C) for 20 minutes. Let cool completely and cut into 24 pieces.

NUTRITIONAL ANALYSIS PER SERVING

- Serving: 1 bar
- Total carbohydrate11 g
- Dietary fiber2 g
- Sodium4 mg
- Saturated fat Minimum amount
- Total fat2 g
- Trans fat0 g
- Cholesterol0 mg
- Protein2 g
- Monounsaturated fat0.5 g
- Calories70
- Added sugars3 g
- Total sugars6 g

34. CREAM AND COOKIE SHAKE

Soy milk is obtained from cooked, crushed and strained soybeans. There is evidence that, if similar animal products are substituted, soy products can lower the risk of heart disease.

INGREDIENTS

- 1 1/3 cups vanilla soy milk (soy milk), cold
- 3 cups fat-free vanilla ice cream
- 6 chocolate wafers, crushed

INSTRUCTIONS

In a blender, mix the soy milk and ice cream. Keep blending until smooth and frothy. Add the cookies and blend a couple of times to mix. Pour the mixture into chilled tall glasses and serve immediately.

NUTRITIONAL ANALYSIS PER SERVING

- Serving: 1 cup (generous)
- Total fat3 g
- Calories270
- Protein9 g
- Cholesterol Minimum amount
- Total carbohydrate52 g
- Dietary fiber11.5 g
- Monounsaturated fat<1 g
- Saturated fat<1 g
- Trans fat0 g
- Sodium224 mg
- Total sugars29 g
- Added sugars11 g

35. ORANGE JUICE SMOOTHIE

For best results, use frozen soy milk and freshly squeezed orange juice.

INGREDIENTS

- 1 1/2 cup orange juice, cold
- 1 cup vanilla soy milk, cold
- 1/3 cup silky or soft tofu
- 1 tablespoon dark honey
- 1 teaspoon grated orange peel
- 1/2 teaspoon vanilla extract
- 5 ice cubes

- 4 peeled orange wedges (about half an orange)

INSTRUCTIONS

In a blender, place the orange set, soy milk, tofu, honey, orange zest, vanilla, and ice cubes. Blend until smooth and frothy, about 30 seconds.

Pour into chilled tall glasses and garnish each glass with an orange wedge.

NUTRITIONAL ANALYSIS PER SERVING

- Serving: 1 cup (8 flow or 240 ml)
- Total carbohydrate20 g
- Dietary fiber1 g
- Sodium40 mg
- Saturated fat<1 g
- Total fat1 g
- Trans fat0 g
- Cholesterol0 mg
- Protein3 g
- Monounsaturated fat<1 g
- Calories101
- Added sugars4 g
- Total sugars14 g

36. BERRIS MARINATED IN BAISAMIC VINGER

For a variation on this recipe, use baby blueberries, gooseberries, and blackberries. Garnish with a sprig of fresh mint.

INGREDIENTS

- 1/4 of Cup of balsamic vinegar
- 2 tablespoons brown sugar
- 1 teaspoon vanilla extract
- 1/2 cup sliced strawberries
- 1/2 cup of blueberries

- 1/2 cup raspberries
- 2 butter rolls

INSTRUCTIONS

In a small bowl, whisk together the balsamic vinegar, brown sugar, and vanilla.

In another bowl, add the strawberries, blueberries, and raspberries. Pour the balsamic vinegar mixture over the berries. Let the fruit marinate for about 10-15 minutes. Drain the marinade.

Place in the refrigerator or serve immediately. To serve, divide the berries among 2 serving dishes. Place the butter roll on the side of the bowl.

Nutritional analysis per serving

- Serving: 3/4 cup
- Calories176
- Total fat4 g
- Saturated fat2 g
- Trans fat0 g
- Monounsaturated fat Minimum amount
- Cholesterol5 g
- Sodium56 mg
- Total carbohydrate33 g
- Dietary fiber4 g
- Added sugars8 g
- Protein2 g

37. ALMOND AND APRICOT BISCOTTI

This double-baked cookie is a classic to accompany with coffee or tea. Whole wheat and walnuts provide the mineral manganese and the antioxidant selenium.

INGREDIENTS

- 3/4 of Cup of bran flour (whole wheat)
- 3/4 of Cup of all-purpose flour (white)
- 1/4 of Cup of brown sugar well packed
- 1 teaspoon of baking powder
- 2 eggs, lightly beaten

- 2 tablespoons 1 percent low-fat milk
- 2 tablespoons canola oil
- 2 tablespoons dark honey
- 1/2 teaspoon of almond extract
- 2/3 cup dried apricots, chopped
- 1/4 cup of large chopped almonds

INSTRUCTIONS

Heat the oven to 350 ° F (175 ° C).

In a large bowl, place the flour, brown sugar, and baking powder. Beat until blended. Add the eggs, milk, canola oil, honey, and almond extract. Stir with a wooden spoon until the dough begins to come together. Add the chopped almonds and apricots. With floured hands, mix the dough until the ingredients are well integrated.

Place the dough on a large sheet of plastic wrap and hand form a flattened roll 12 inches (30 cm) long, 3 inches (7.5 cm) wide and about 1 inch (2.5 cm) High. Lift the plastic wrap and invert the dough onto a nonstick cookie sheet. Bake for 25 to 30 minutes, until lightly browned. Transfer it to another cookie sheet and let it cool for 10 minutes. Leave the oven at 350 ° F (175 ° C).

Place the chilled dough on a cutting board. Using a serrated knife, cut crosswise into 24 1/2-inch-wide slices. Place the slices cut side down on the cookie sheet. Bake again for 15-20 minutes, until crisp. Transfer to a rack and allow to cool completely. Store in an airtight container.

NUTRITIONAL ANALYSIS PER SERVING

Serving: 1 cookie
Calories75
Total fat2 g
Saturated fat Minimum amount
Trans fat Minimum amount
Monounsaturated fat1 g
Cholesterol15 mg
Sodium17 mg
Total carbohydrate12 g
Dietary fiber1 g
Total sugars6 g
Added sugars2 g
Protein2 g

38. APPLE SCONE

Use baked pie apples like Granny Smith, R. I. Greening, or Northern Spy.

INGREDIENTS

- Mass:
- 1 tablespoon butter
- 1 teaspoon of honey
- 1 cup whole wheat flour
- 2 tablespoons of buckwheat flour
- 2 tablespoons oat flakes
- 2 tablespoons brandy or apple liqueur
- Stuffing the buns:
- 6 large tart apples, thinly sliced
- 1 teaspoon of nutmeg

- 2 tablespoons of honey
- Peel of a lemon

Instructions

Heat the oven to 350 ° F (175 ° C).

Combine the butter, honey, flours, and oats in a food processor. Pulse several times, until the mixture looks finely crushed. Add brandy or apple liqueur and pulse a few more times, until the mixture begins to form a bun. Remove the mixture from the food processor, wrap tightly in a plastic bag, and refrigerate for two hours.

Mix the apples, nutmeg, and honey. Add the lemon zest. Reservation.

Roll out the chilled dough, with an additional amount of flour, to a 1/4 inch (0.5 cm) thickness. Cut into 8-inch (20 cm) circles. Use an 8-cup aluminum muffin pan and lightly spray the pan with cooking spray. Place a circle of dough on each cavity drizzled with oil. Press the dough gently. Fill with the apple mixture. Fold the dough on the sides and press on the top to seal. Bake for 30 minutes at 350 ° F (175 ° C) or until golden brown.

NUTRITIONAL ANALYSIS PER SERVING

- Portion: 1 bun
- Calories178
- Total fat2.5 g
- Saturated fat1 g
- Trans fat Minimum amount
- Monounsaturated fat0.5 g
- Cholesterol4 mg
- Sodium14 mg
- Total carbohydrate36 g

- Dietary fiber6 g
- Added sugars5 g
- Protein3 g

39. RICE PUDDING WITH FRUITS

Make this Fruit Rice Pudding ahead of time, store it in the fridge and serve it cold. You can also serve this dessert warm, fresh from the oven.

INGREDIENTS

- 2 cups of water
- 1 cup long grain brown rice
- 4 cups nonfat evaporated milk
- 1/2 cup of brown sugar
- 1/2 teaspoon lemon zest
- 1 teaspoon vanilla extract
- 6 egg whites
- 1/4 of Cup of pineapple crushed
- 1/4 cup of raisins
- 1/4 cup dried apricots, chopped

Instructions

In a medium saucepan, bring 2 cups of water to a boil. Add the rice and cook it for 10 minutes. Pour into a colander and drain well.

In the same saucepan, add the evaporated milk and brown sugar. Cook until hot. Add the cooked rice, lemon zest, and vanilla extract. Cook over low heat until mixture thickens and rice is tender, about 30 minutes. Remove from the fire and let cool.

In a small bowl, beat the egg whites. Pour them into the rice mixture. Add the pineapple, raisins, and apricots. Stir until the ingredients are well integrated.

Heat the oven to 325 ° F (160 ° C). Lightly coat a baking dish with cooking spray. Spoon pudding and fruit mixture into baking dish. Bake about 20 minutes until the pudding is hard. Serve warm or cold.

Nutritional analysis per serving

- Serving size: about 1/2 cup
- Calories257
- Total fat1 g
- Saturated fat<0.5 g
- Trans fat0 g
- Monounsaturated fat<0.5 g
- Cholesterol5 mg
- Sodium193 mg
- Total carbohydrate48 g
- Dietary fiber1 g
- Added sugars9 g
- Protein17 g

40. FRUIT COMPOTE WITH ICE CREAM

Half a cup of this fruit compote provides 2 servings of fruit.

INGREDIENTS

- 1 1/4 cup of water
- 1/2 cup unsweetened orange juice
- 1 12-ounce (340g) package mixed dried fruit (cuts large fruit cubes)
- 1 teaspoon ground cinnamon
- 1/4 teaspoon ground nutmeg
- 1/4 teaspoon ground ginger
- 4 cups fat free vanilla frozen yogurt

INSTRUCTIONS

Combine the water, orange juice, dried fruit, cinnamon, nutmeg, and ginger in a saucepan and cook over medium heat. Stir gently and cook covered over low heat for 10 minutes.

Uncover and continue simmering on very low heat for 10 more minutes or until fruit is soft.

Serve warm or cold in bowls with vanilla frozen yogurt.

NUTRITIONAL ANALYSIS PER SERVING

- Serving: 1/2 cup compote and 1/2 cup frozen yogurt
- Total carbohydrate47 g
- Dietary fiber5 g
- Sodium68 mg
- Saturated fat Minimum amount
- Total fat Minimum amount
- Trans fat0 g
- Cholesterol3 mg
- Protein5 g
- Monounsaturated fat Minimum amount
- Calories208
- Added sugars4 g
- Total sugars33 g

41. STRAWBERRY CREAM CHEESE CREPES

If you use whipped cream cheese in these crepes instead of regular cream cheese, you save a third of the calories, fat, and sodium. The recipe can be prepared with other berries and also with stone fruits, such as peaches or apricots, sliced.

INGREDIENTS

- 4 tablespoons cream cheese, softened
- 2 tablespoons sifted powdered sugar
- 2 teaspoons vanilla extract
- 2 packaged crepes, about 8 inches (20 cm) in diameter each
- 8 fresh strawberries, sliced and stems removed

- 1 teaspoon of powdered sugar to decorate
- 2 tablespoons caramel sauce, warm

INSTRUCTIONS

Heat the oven to 325 ° F (160 ° C). Lightly coat a baking dish with cooking spray.

In a bowl, mix the cream cheese until smooth using an electric mixer. Add the powdered sugar and vanilla. Mix well.

Spread half of the cream cheese mixture on each crepe, leaving a 1/2-inch border. Top with 2 tablespoons of strawberries. Roll up and place the fold upside down in the prepared baking dish. Bake until lightly browned, about 10 minutes.

Cut the crepes in half. Arrange them on four individual plates. Sprinkle with powdered sugar and top with 1/2 tablespoon of caramel sauce. Serve immediately.

NUTRITIONAL ANALYSIS PER SERVING

- Serving: 1/2 crepe
- Total carbohydrate17 g
- Dietary fiber0.5 g
- Sodium161 mg
- Saturated fat4 g
- Total fat7 g
- Trans fat Minimum amount
- Cholesterol37 mg
- Protein3 g
- Monounsaturated fat0.5 g
- Calories143
- Total sugars11 g
- Added sugars7 g

42. CRUCHY ALMONDS AND APRICOTS

This apricot dessert is flourless and gluten-free if made with gluten-free oatmeal.

Ingredients

- 1 teaspoon of olive oil
- 1-pound (450g) apricots, halved and pitted
- 1/2 cup almonds, chopped
- 1 tablespoon oatmeal (certified gluten-free)
- 1 teaspoon anise seeds
- 2 tablespoons of honey

INSTRUCTIONS

Heat the oven to 350 ° F (175 ° C).

Brush a 9-inch (23 cm) glass cake pan with olive oil. Chop the apricots and place them in a cake tin. Sprinkle the almonds, oatmeal and anise seeds on top. Drizzle with honey.

Bake for 25 minutes, until the almond coating is golden brown and the apricots are bubbly. Serve warm.

NUTRITIONAL ANALYSIS PER SERVING

- Serving size: about 1/2 cup
- Calories134
- Total fat6 g
- Saturated fat0.5 g
- Trans fat Minimum amount
- Monounsaturated fat4
- Cholesterol0 mg
- Sodium1 mg
- Total carbohydrate17 g
- Dietary fiber3 g
- Added sugars6 g
- Protein3 g

43. STRAWBERRIES AND CREAM

Strawberries are a good source of vitamin C and potassium. Here they're paired with amaretto liqueur and fat-free sour cream for a low-fat dessert.

INGREDIENTS

- 1 1/2 cup fat-free sour cream
- 1/2 cup of brown sugar
- 2 tablespoons amaretto liqueur
- 1 quart (about a liter) fresh strawberries, stemmed and cut in half (save 6 whole for garnish)

INSTRUCTIONS

In a small bowl, combine the fat-free sour cream, brown sugar, and liqueur.

In a large bowl, add the halved strawberries and sour cream mixture. Stir gently to mix. Cover and refrigerate until chilled, about 1 hour.

Spoon the strawberries into 6 colored bowls or chilled sherbet glasses. Garnish with whole strawberries and serve immediately.

NUTRITIONAL ANALYSIS PER SERVING

- Serving: 2/3 cup approximately
- Total carbohydrate31 g
- Dietary fiber2 g
- Sodium95 mg
- Saturated fat Minimum amount
- Total fat Minimum amount
- Trans fat Minimum amount
- Cholesterol6 mg
- Protein3 g
- Monounsaturated fat Minimum amount
- Calories136
- Total sugars18 g
- Added sugars11 g

44. GRILLED FRUIT

Roasting the fruit caramelizes the natural sugar in it, browning the sugar and intensifying the sweetness of the fruit.

INGREDIENTS

- 1 small pineapple, peeled, cored and cut into 4 chunks
- 2 large mangoes, cored and cut in half
- 2 large peaches, cored and cut in half
- Butter flavored cooking spray
- 2 tablespoons brown sugar
- 1/2 cup balsamic vinegar
- Fresh mint or basil for garnish

INSTRUCTIONS

In a large bowl, place the pineapple, mangoes, and peaches. Spray generously with cooking spray. Stir and drizzle again so the fruit is well coated. Sprinkle with brown sugar. Stir until everything is evenly coated. Reservation.

In a small saucepan, heat the balsamic vinegar over low heat. Cook over low heat until the liquid is reduced by half, stirring occasionally. Remove from the heat.

Build a fire in a charcoal grill or heat a gas grill or rotisserie. Away from heat source, lightly coat grill or grill with cooking spray. Place the cooking grate 4 to 6 inches (10 to 15 cm) from the heat source.

Place the fruit on the grill or roasting pan. Grill or broil over medium heat until sugar is caramelized, about 3 to 5 minutes.

Remove the fruit from the grill and place it on individual plates. Drizzle with balsamic vinegar and garnish with mint or basil. Serve immediately.

NUTRITIONAL ANALYSIS PER SERVING

- Serving: 3 units of roasted fruits and sauce
- Total fat<1 g
- Calories264
- Protein3 g
- Cholesterolo mg
- Total carbohydrate63 g
- Dietary fiber3 g

- Monounsaturated fat Minimum amount
- Saturated fat Minimum amount
- Trans fat Minimum amount
- Sodium11 mg
- Added sugars4 g
- Total sugars52 g

45.SUMMER FUIRT AND GRATIN

Although a pitted summer fruit mix is used in this recipe, it can be easily adapted. In early summer, use raspberries and apricots. In fall, you can combine apples and blueberries.

INGREDIENTS

For the filling:

- 1-pound (450g) cherries, pitted, cut in half
- 4 cups of summer fruits, such as nectarines, peaches and apricots, peeled, pitted, sliced
- 1 tablespoon whole wheat flour
- 1 tablespoon turbinado sugar or well packed light brown sugar
- For the coating:

- 1/2 cup of traditional rolled oats
- 1/4 cup sliced almonds (flakes)
- 3 tablespoons whole wheat flour
- 2 tablespoons turbinado sugar or well packed light brown sugar
- 1/4 teaspoon ground cinnamon
- 1/8 of teaspoon of ground nutmeg
- 1/8 teaspoon of salt
- 2 tablespoons walnut oil or canola oil
- 1 tablespoon dark honey

INSTRUCTIONS

Heat the oven to 350 ° F (175 ° C). Lightly coat a 9-inch (23 cm) square baking dish with cooking spray. In a bowl, mix the cherry tomatoes and seasonal fruits. Sprinkle with the flour and turbinado sugar and stir gently to integrate the ingredients.

To prepare the topping, mix the oats, almonds, flour, turbinado sugar, cinnamon, nutmeg and salt in another bowl. Beat until blended. Add the oil and honey, and mix until the ingredients are well integrated.

Spread the fruit mixture evenly in the prepared baking dish. Drizzle the oatmeal and almond mixture evenly over the fruits. Bake the fruits for 45 to 55 minutes, until they are bubbly and the topping is slightly golden. Serve hot or at room temperature.

Nutritional analysis per serving

- Serving: About 3/4 cup
- Total carbohydrate39 g
- Dietary fiber5 g
- Sodium56 mg

- Saturated fat0.5 g
- Total fat7 g
- Cholesterol0 mg
- Protein4 g
- Monounsaturated fat4 g
- Calories235
- Trans fat Minimum amount
- Total sugars25 g
- Added sugars9 g

46. APPLE WITH SAUCE

Using fat-free cream cheese instead of full-fat cream cheese cuts about 50 calories and 4 grams of mostly saturated fat from each serving.

INGREDIENTS

- 8 ounces (225g) fat free cream cheese
- 2 tablespoons brown sugar
- 1 1/2 teaspoon vanilla
- 2 tablespoons ground peanuts without salt
- 4 medium or 8 small apples, hollowed and sliced
- 1/2 cup of orange juice

INSTRUCTIONS

Remove the cream cheese from the refrigerator to soften, about 5 minutes.

In a small bowl, combine the brown sugar, vanilla, and cream cheese. Mix until smooth. Add the chopped peanuts and stir.

Place the apple slices in another bowl. Drizzle orange juice over the apples so they don't brown. Drain the sliced apples and serve with the sauce.

NUTRITIONAL ANALYSIS PER SERVING

- Serving size: 1/2 medium apple and 2 tablespoons sauce
- Total carbohydrate19 g
- Dietary fiber2.5 g
- Sodium202 mg
- Saturated fat0.5 g
- Trans fat0 g
- Total fat2 g
- Cholesterol3 mg
- Protein6 g
- Monounsaturated fat1 g
- Calories118
- Added sugars3 g
- Total sugars15 g

47. BAKED APPLE WITH CHERRIES AND ALMONDS

Any apple suitable for baking, such as Golden Delicious, Rome or Granny Smith, retains its shape perfectly for this dish.

INGREDIENTS

- 1/3 cup dried cherries, chopped large
- 3 tablespoons of chopped almonds
- 1 tablespoon of wheat germ
- 1 tablespoon packed brown sugar
- 1/2 teaspoon ground cinnamon
- 1/8 of teaspoon of ground nutmeg
- 6 small golden delicious apples, approx. 1 3/4 pound (800 g) total
- 1/2 cup apple juice

- 1/4 cup of water
- 2 tablespoons dark honey
- 2 teaspoons walnut oil or canola oil

INSTRUCTIONS

Preheat the oven to 350 ° F (175 ° C).

In a small bowl, mix the cherries, almonds, wheat germ, brown sugar, cinnamon, and nutmeg until all ingredients are evenly distributed. Reservation.

Apples can be left skin on, if you wish. To decoratively peel the apples, with a peeler or sharp knife, remove the skin from each apple in a circular motion, leaving a strip in between, alternating a strip of skin with a strip of apple pulp. Core apples from the stem, stopping 3/4 inch from the base.

Divide the cherry mixture evenly among the apples, gently pressing the mixture into each cavity. Place the apples side up in a heavy ovenproof skillet or small baking dish just the right size for the apples. Pour the apple juice and water into the fountain. Drizzle the honey and oil over the apples, evenly, and cover the dish with aluminum foil so that it is snug. Bake until apples are tender when pierced with a knife, 50 to 60 minutes.

Transfer the apples to individual plates and drizzle with the juices from the platter. Serve hot or at room temperature.

Nutritional analysis per serving

- Serving: 1 apple
- Calories200
- Total fat4 g
- Saturated fat0 g
- Trans fat0 g
- Monounsaturated fat2 g

- Cholesterol0 mg
- Sodium7 mg
- Total carbohydrate39 g
- Dietary fiber5 g
- Total sugars31 g
- Added sugars8 g
- Protein2 g

48. RHUBARBS AND PECAN MUFFINS

While pecans are high in calories and fat, sprinkling some over these muffins helps achieve a crunchy texture and unmistakable flavor. Pecans are also a good source of fiber and nutrients like thiamine and copper.

Ingredients

- 1 cup all-purpose flour (white)
- 1 cup bran flour (whole wheat)
- 1/2 cup of sugar
- 1 1/2 teaspoons of baking powder
- 1/2 teaspoon of baking soda
- 1/2 teaspoon salt
- 2 egg whites
- 2 tablespoons canola oil
- 2 tablespoons unsweetened applesauce

- 2 teaspoons grated orange peel
- 3/4 cup calcium-fortified orange juice
- 1 1/4 cup rhubarb, finely chopped
- 2 tablespoons chopped pecans

INSTRUCTIONS

Preheat the oven to 350 ° F (175 ° C). Cover a muffin pan with foil or foil wrappers.

In a large bowl, combine the flours, sugar, baking powder, baking soda, and salt. Stir to mix well.

In a separate bowl, add the egg whites, canola oil, applesauce, and orange zest and juice. Beat with an electric mixer until smooth. Add to flour mixture and mix just until moistened, but still lumpy. Add the chopped rhubarb.

Spoon batter into 12 muffin wrappers and fill about 2/3 of each. Sprinkle 1/2 teaspoon chopped pecans on each muffin and bake for about 25-30 minutes until fluffy to the touch. Let cool for 5 minutes; then transfer the muffins to a wire rack to cool completely.

NUTRITIONAL ANALYSIS PER SERVING

- Serving: 1 muffin
- Cholesterol0 mg
- Calories143
- Sodium190 mg
- Total fat3 g
- Total carbohydrate26 g
- Saturated fat<1 g
- Dietary fiber2 g
- Trans fat Minimum amount
- Added sugars8 g
- Monounsaturated fat2 g
- Protein3 g

49. Whole Wheat Banana Bread

This whole wheat bread is also gluten free. Wheat flour is replaced with rice, amaranth, millet, quinoa and tapioca flours.

Ingredients

- 1/2 cup of brown rice flour
- 1/2 cup of amaranth flour
- 1/2 cup tapioca flour
- 1/2 of Cup of millet flour
- 1/2 cup quinoa flour
- 1 teaspoon of baking soda
- 1/2 teaspoon of baking powder
- 1/8 teaspoon of salt

- 3/4 cup egg substitute (or use egg whites)
- 2 tablespoons grapeseed oil
- 1/2 cup raw sugar
- 2 cups of mashed banana

INSTRUCTIONS

Heat the oven to 350 ° F (175 ° C). Prepare a 5 × 9-inch (13 × 23 cm) loaf pan by lightly spraying it with cooking spray. Sprinkle with a little of any of the used flours. Reservation. In a large bowl, mix all the ingredients except the sugar. In a separate bowl, mix the egg, oil, sugar, and banana puree. Mix well. Add the wet mix to the dry ingredients and mix well. With a spoon, spoon the mixture into a loaf pan. Bake for 50 to 60 minutes.

Check the doneness with a toothpick; when the toothpick is removed it should not have any mixture stuck to it. Take the bread out of the oven, let it cool, cut it up and serve it.

NUTRITIONAL ANALYSIS PER SERVING

- Serving: 1 slice
- Total carbohydrate30 g
- Dietary fiber2 g
- Sodium146 mg
- Saturated fat0.5 g
- Total fat3 g
- Trans fat0 g
- Cholesterol0 mg
- Protein4 g
- Monounsaturated fat0.5 g
- Calories163
- Added sugars7 g
- Total sugars10 g

50. QUICK CARROT SPICE BREAD

Quick breads are very easy to make. In this recipe, fruits are used to sweeten the preparation and carrots to give it a tender texture. Also, carrots make this bread an excellent source of vitamin A.

INGREDIENTS

- 1/2 cup sifted all-purpose flour
- 1 cup whole wheat flour
- 2 teaspoons baking powder
- 1/2 teaspoon baking soda
- 1/2 teaspoon ground cinnamon
- 1/4 teaspoon ground ginger
- 1/3 cup margarine without trans fats, softened to room temperature

- 1/4 cup, plus 2 tablespoons packed brown sugar
- 1/3 cup skim milk
- 2 tablespoons unsweetened orange juice
- 2 egg whites, or 1 egg substitute, shake
- 1 teaspoon vanilla extract
- 1 teaspoon grated orange peel
- 1 1/2 cup grated carrots
- 2 tablespoons golden raisins
- 1 tablespoon walnuts, finely chopped

INSTRUCTIONS

Heat the oven to 375 ° F (190 ° C). Spray a 2 1/2 × 4 1/2 × 8 1/2-inch (6.5 × 12 × 22 cm) loaf pan with cooking spray.

In a small bowl, mix the first 6 dry ingredients. Reservation.

Using a mixer, or stirring vigorously by hand, make a cream with the margarine and sugar in a large bowl. Whisk together the milk, orange juice, egg, vanilla, and orange zest. Stir in the carrots, raisins, and walnuts. Add the reserved dry ingredients. Mix well.

With a spoon, spoon the mixture into a loaf pan. Bake for 45 minutes or until a toothpick inserted in the center comes out clean. Let cool in pan for 10 minutes. Remove from the mold and cool completely on a wire rack.

Nutritional analysis per serving

- Portion: 1/2-inch (1 cm) slice
- Total carbohydrate15 g
- Dietary fiber1 g

- Sodium82 mg
- Saturated fat1 g
- Total fat5 g
- Trans fat0 g
- Cholesterol minimum amountProtein2 g
- Monounsaturated fat2 g
- Calories110
- Added sugars6 g

CONCLUSION

There are many reasons to move to sugar-free diets, health benefits between them. However, there is still a risk. Sugar-free food is inherently good for you. These foods are generally better for you than alternatives filled with sugar, but that doesn't mean they are healthy. This can cheat sometimes because there is a perception that eating more nutritious food will lead to a healthier lifestyle. While this is overall, moderation still needs to be practiced. Diet rules must always be obeyed. Be sure to find balance in this type of food because too many good things can cause problems.

CPSIA information can be obtained
at www.ICGtesting.com
Printed in the USA
BVHW092256250521
608096BV00004B/268